So, You Want to Become a National Board Certified Teacher?

So, You Want to Become a National Board Certified Teacher?

A Handbook of Teacher Tips for Successfully Completing the *NBPTS* Certification

Jerry L. Parks, Ed.S., NBCT

Weekly Reader Press
New York Lincoln Shanghai

So, You Want to Become a National Board Certified Teacher?
A Handbook of Teacher Tips for Successfully Completing the
NBPTS Certification

Copyright © 2004 by Jerry Parks

Weekly Reader Press
an imprint of iUniverse, Inc.
and the Weekly Reader Corporation

iUniverse books may be ordered through booksellers or by contacting:

iUniverse
2021 Pine Lake Road, Suite 100
Lincoln, NE 68512
www.iuniverse.com
1-800-Authors (1-800-288-4677)

ISBN-13: 978-0-595-32728-7
ISBN-10: 0-595-32728-1

Printed in the United States of America

Contents

Preface to the Second Edition

In the year since the first edition of this book was released, numerous NBCT's graciously offered suggestions for improvement. This second edition—completely revised, updated, and expanded—is the result of those efforts.

In addition, the self-test for readiness has been re-weighed for better accuracy, the list of 'buzzwords' has been expanded, a sample list of documented accomplishments has been included, and the instructions for writing have been clarified.

The *NBPTS* certification process is a daunting endeavor. As beneficial and validating as it may be, obtaining this certification is difficult, time-consuming, and challenging. This book is designed to offer successfully proven strategies to help the aspiring teacher avoid many of the pitfalls of the 50–75% first-time failure rate. The work is the compilation of suggestions, not only from the author, but also from countless other *NBPTS* candidates, and certified teachers.

Most teachers already do an excellent job in the classroom, nevertheless, more and more states are encouraging *NBPTS* certification. Teachers should, and will, validate their successes if they are able to pass the rigors of the *NBPTS* portfolios and testing.

National Board certification not only validates excellent teaching, it also reflects excellent teaching. According to research provided by the *NBPTS*, board certified teachers outperformed their peers in 11 of 13 key dimensions of teaching. They were more adept at recognizing why students succeeded or failed on academic tasks, engaging students, and improvising when faced with unexpected occurrences.

The *NBPTS* certification process is the same regardless of which certification area is chosen. Candidates prepare a portfolio, to be completed in a classroom, which reflects detailed analyses of their teaching practice. The portfolio is comprised of videotapes of the candidate's teaching and student interaction, analyzed student learning samples, and teacher artifacts reflecting documented accomplishments. The portfolio is graded by trained assessors, and based on a rubric of *National Standards* within the content area.

Candidates are then required to attend an Assessment Center where they are tested over questions reflecting content knowledge within specific content areas. In order to certify, the candidate must complete all required portfolio entries, the assessment exam, and score a minimum total of 275 points. Certification is then valid for ten years, after which there is a renewal process.

There is no one right way to gain certification. Let me repeat, there is no one *right* way to pass. Utilizing tips and helps from those who have gone through the process can greatly enhance a candidate's chance of obtaining certification. But experiences and advice can and will differ.

Much of the material presented will seem redundant. Many suggestions are cited over and over, and in different sections. This repetition is intentional in order to emphasize important points as well as keep those points before the eyes of the reader.

Information presented was current as of the publication date. Some information is state-specific, and certificate areas are continually being added. More detailed information is available from http://www.nbpts.org/. This book is in no way connected with the *National Board for Professional Teaching Standards* or its affiliates, and represents solely the opinions of the author.

Chapter 1

Do I really want to do this?

(General requirements, and my self-evaluation)

Do I have a good reason?

OK, so you're considering the *NBPTS* process, are you? Hmm, why are you doing this? Let's see, do any of the following (typical) reasons sound familiar?

- Others have told me I really ought to give this a shot!

- I've been thinking about this for a long time, and I probably should just go for it!

- I could use the extra money certification brings!

- To be honest, the recognition would be really nice!

- I really love a challenge! When I heard the process was tough, I knew I had to try!

- I want to become a better teacher!

- I could benefit from an accepted citation of accomplished teaching that is transferable between states.

- I *am* an accomplished teacher, and I want to *prove* it!

- I really would like to become 'qualified' to help other teachers improve.

- I want to use this to move up to a higher position.

- My best friend certified, and if *they* can do—I can do it!

- I've got too much time on my hands! (*OK, forget this one!*)

Am I eligible to pursue certification?

In order to pursue *NBPTS* certification, there are three main requirements (which you will be required to verify):

❑ You must have at least a baccalaureate degree from an accredited institution

❑ You must have at least three years of teaching experience in a k-12 setting

❑ You must hold a valid teaching license

Am I showing symptoms of what it takes to do it?

These are among the many reasons you may be considering *National Board Certification*. Whatever your reasons are, compare them against some these characteristics below. I like to call these my *National Board Personality Traits for Success*. You may not 'suffer' all the symptoms, but if you don't have *several*, you might not be quite ready to tackle the certification process. See how you do:

✓ I enjoy *ladder climbing*, which is pushing myself to find the limits of my skills!

✓ I'm really a 'closet lawyer'—I love searching for evidence to establish a point!

✓ I actually *enjoy* professional development and attending local, state, and national conferences!

✓ I enjoy technology, and working on a computer is actually *fun* for me!

✓ As a teacher, I believe that *application, application, and application* are the three most important goals of a taught lesson!

✓ I honestly see my students as *individuals first*, and as *students* second.

✓ I am very task-oriented, fairly organized, and have a *'get this done'* attitude, and others call me *'anal retentive!'*

✓ I like to write, have a broad vocabulary, and people have told me I have a *'way with words.'*

✓ I have fun taking timed quizzes in my spare time.

✓ I am a community-oriented person.

✓ I enjoy *variety* in my teaching methods, and am always game to try something new!

✓ I have a solid support group of family, and/or friends.

✓ Challenges *stimulate*—not discourage—me.

✓ I think assessing is cool, and continually assess *myself* as well as my students!

The least I need to know!

So, how did you do? If you find yourself coming down with many of the symptoms of what it takes to complete the process of *NBPTS* certification, let's be sure you understand the pitfalls you could face.

First, realize this is a *long-term commitment*. It generally takes about 300–400 hours to complete the certification process. At least that's the estimate. If you can't 'marry' the thing for six months—don't get 'engaged'!

Second, you must possess at least a baccalaureate degree from an accredited institution, hold a valid teaching license, and have access to a classroom.

Third, understand that you must have a *minimum* of three full years in the classroom (not necessarily in the same school). A minimum of *five* is generally recommended. *Experience counts.* The *NBPTS* is looking for accomplished teachers who are still learning. That's the bottom line.

Fourth, if you leave your certification area, you will likely lose whatever stipend your are receiving for certifying. Choose a certification area in which you plan on remaining.

Finally, know that approximately 42% of the candidates certify on their first attempt. *You get three attempts.* If you don't pass the first time, you can become a 'banker', or 'advanced candidate'. Approximately 86% of advanced candidates retry, and around 63% of these eventually make it. Remember—when you certify, it won't matter one whit whether you did it on the first, second or third attempt! *Consider certification as a one to three year process.*

Still game?

Let's quantify all this to find out just how ready you are. Take this little inventory analysis. *No cheating! Don't look at the scale at the end before you take it!* Answer each of the following statements as honestly as you can using the following rating terms. Circle the number under the category that most describes you. I have weighted some categories according to importance. **Feel free to use 'in between' numbers if you want.** When you finish, add your total. *Remember—no cheating!*

Definitely	*Probably*	*Questionable*	*No, not really!*

1. I can deal with *extra* planning, organization, and deadlines.

8	6	2	0

2. I am *adept* at identifying student needs and the objectives necessary to meet them.

9	6	2	0

3. I am *familiar* with the *National Standards* in my teaching area.

9	6	4	0

4. I make a *conscious* effort to address diversity, encourage risk-taking, and treat all my students equally.

9	6	3	0

5. I can cite and fully document at least three professional accomplishments in my career that *impact student learning.*

9	7	4	0

6. I am able to 'write tight' *clearly, convincingly,* and *persuasively.*

9	6	3	0

7. I have 300–400 extra hours to spare in order to devote to this process.

8	6	2	0

8. I can think 'outside the box', and I use a *variety* of teaching strategies in my classroom.

6	4	2	0

9. I understand and utilize the *multiple intelligences* in my classroom.

8	6	3	0

10. I go *beyond* the normal expectations of teachers in establishing and maintaining *two-way communication* with parents.

9	7	3	0

11. I am self-motivated, and a self-starter whom my colleagues would call *task oriented.*

8	5	3	0

12. I can afford to pay the approximately $2500 to begin the process.

   9   7   3   0

13. I know how to *analyze, interpret,* and *reflect upon* information, and know what these terms really mean!

   9   6   3   0

14. I have the emotional support from family, friends, and school administration to strengthen me during a yearlong endeavor.

   7   5   3   0

15. I know how to make relevant and practical *real-world application* of my lessons to my students' lives, and I do it on a *regular* basis.

   9   6   4   0

16. I can document at least one or two ways in which my community involvement has *evidenced student learning.*

   8   5   3   0

17. I *sincerely* consider my personal failures merely an opportunity to improve!

   9   6   4   0

16. I have conducted workshops, in-services, or similar professional development activities more than once at the local, state or national level.

   9   7   2   0

17. I *regularly* reflect upon my successes and failures, and I modify lessons accordingly.

   8   6   3   0

18. I can handle personal constructive criticism regarding my writing style and teaching practice—even in group settings.

   9   7   3   0

19. I go *beyond* the basic grading procedures in evaluating my students, and often use rubrics and multiple methods of feedback.

   9   6   3   0

20. I really *want* to understand the backgrounds and home lives of my students, in order to put a *perspective* on how they learn.

   7   5   3   0

21. I am willing and able to travel a reasonable distance in order to work with a mentor, and/or attend mentor cohort meetings.

   8   6   2   0

22. I know how to *effectively* utilize cooperative learning opportunities.

    9   6   3   0

23. I enjoy collaborating with my colleagues in developing and implementing instructional activities.

    9   5   3   0

24. I *enjoy* videotaping and watching with my students various activities of learning!

    5   3   1   0

25. I actually enjoy working at a computer, and have little difficulty with word processing skills.

    8   5   2   0

26. I can maintain a 'bounce-back' attitude without becoming unduly discouraged.

    8   5   2   0

27. I have no problem asking for help when I feel inadequate, and I will search till I find an answer when necessary!

    9   6   3   0

My total _____

Although this little inventory analysis is not an official, or guaranteed accurate measure of your ability to attain *NBPTS* certification, if you scored much below 180, you might consider whether or not now is the right time to sacrifice the next six months of your life to the hard work certification entails. Just something to think about.

The benefits of National Board Certification:

✓ Around 2% of all teachers in the United States are certified.

✓ The *NBPTS* advances reform in all states and standardizes certification between states.

✓ Certification addressed *No Child Left Behind* legislation in assuring that teachers are Highly Qualified Educators.

✓ In a study, 75% of students taught by NBCT's demonstrated higher levels of concept comprehension compared to 30% of students taught by non-*National Board* certified teachers.

✓ Research shows that being taught by an NBCT is equal to an average of an extra month of school.

✓ National Board certification reshapes the public perception of education. It is the one universally accepted valid indicator of teaching excellence.

✓ Students of NBCT's experienced year-end testing improvements averaging between 7–15% more than peers whose teachers were not NBCT's.

Surveys have shown that:

• 92% of NBPTS candidates believe they are better teachers as a result of participating in the process.

• 80% report collaboration with colleagues leads to more focused teaching and learning.

• 89% improved their evaluation of student learning.

Misconceptions regarding National Board Certification:

1. You need to be the model teacher to succeed in the process.
   No, you need to be an effective teacher who is willing to learn to be a better one.

2. You should choose your brightest students and your finest lesson to use for your portfolio.
   Not necessarily. The NBPTS is looking for improvement *in both your teaching and student learning.*

3. You should not mention in your writing those things which go wrong in your classroom lessons.
   Truth is, how you address, analyze, and correct such occurrences provides a wonderful avenue for expressing how you learn as a teacher.

4. Assessors may be out of your subject area, and unable to evaluate your work in an expert manner.
   Truth: You will be evaluated by more than one assessor who is skilled in your subject area, and a standard deviation for error will be figured in to eliminate any possibility of statistical error.

5. You have only one attempt at certification.
   Truth: You may retake any portfolio or assessment center entry (with a score of 2.74 or less) up to two more times within 24 months from when you first receive your scores.

6. If you retake entries, only your highest score counts.
   Truth: Your retake score is always the score of record—even if it's lower. If you plan to retake more than 7 entries/exercises, you may want to consider applying to repeat the National Board Certification assessment in its entirety. Reapplying and taking the assessment from the beginning, rather than taking 8, 9, or 10 entries/exercises this year, will reduce your overall fee.

7. If you retake your certification process, you must still be teaching in the same area of your initial certification in order to qualify.
   Truth: You may 'borrow' a classroom to complete your original certification category, as long as the subject content and student ages qualify. Documented accomplishments, however, may be used from a new, or original setting.

Chapter 2

The *NBPTS* Proposition & Core Content

(Accomplished teachers, the Core & more!)

OK, the bottom line.

To put it in a nutshell, the *NBPTS* is looking for accomplished teachers who are still learning.

These are teachers who go *above and beyond* what the average teacher does. What does above and beyond mean? It means a conscious and deliberate effort by a teacher to do *more* than what is expected as a part of the typical teaching routine.

Here's what the *NBPTS* expects of you. The *NBPTS Core Propositions* expect that accomplished teachers (teachers who perform *above and beyond* what is expected of every teacher) should be skilled in five areas. These are:

Commitment to your students. In helping to accomplish this, you must:

❑ Emphasize equality

❑ Recognize diversity

❑ Effectively motivate

❑ Be familiar with child development theories

❑ Sufficiently challenge

❑ Recognize unique learning styles

❑ Understand backgrounds

❑ Address interests and needs

Accomplished teachers maximize instruction based on what students bring from their world into the classroom. Accomplished teachers generalize content for students to take back to the real world. Accomplished teachers create a stimulating learning environment, and understand that school is so much more than academics.

Knowledge of your subject. This includes:

❑ Real-world application

❑ Encouraging lifelong learning

❑ Lesson relevancy

❑ Technology integration

❑ *National Standards* based content

❑ Formulation of critical thinking questions

❑ Recognizing the importance of interdisciplinary teaching

Accomplished teachers create student-friendly classrooms and facilitate student-centered learning. The knowledge of an accomplished teacher is not merely broad—it is deep. Accomplished teachers challenge through critical thinking and understand the importance of lesson application.

Management and monitoring your students' learning. This includes:

❑ Your classroom environment

❑ Setting expectations

❑ Reaching reluctant learners

❑ Encouraging involvement and risk-taking

❑ Student interaction and engagement

❑ Goal setting

❑ Assessment

Accomplished teachers squeeze teaching minutes for all they're worth. Accomplished teachers have a plan for their instruction, and know how to differ assessment techniques. Accomplished teachers do not merely teach information, they teach how to learn. They know where they want to take their students and what it requires to get there!

Reflection on your personal teaching practice. This includes:

❑ You as a role-model of leadership

❑ You as a lifetime learner

❑ You as a model of *best practices*

Accomplished teachers are pragmatists—they use what works! They know how to sift information down to what's really important. Accomplished teachers know how to make objectives bloom, and how to research and modify whenever necessary.

You as part of the community. This includes:

❑ How you deal with parents

❑ How you deal with the business community

❑ How you collaborate with other teachers

❑ How you utilize technology

Accomplished teachers know they do not teach in isolation. They are a part of a greater whole. Accomplished teachers understand the importance of sharing the load and learning from—and teaching—others along the way.

Bottom line: "An NBCT should be able to demonstrate through demanding performance assessment what an accomplished teacher should know and be able to do."

Keep in mind, the certification *process* is the same *regardless* of the area in which you choose to certify.

Chapter 3

The organization and scoring
of the material

(The nuts & bolts of it all!)

The make-up of the portfolio

Although the format can differ slightly, basically, there are 400 possible 'scaled score' points that you can earn. These points are weighted. Your portfolio, that is, what you get in your box—the four entries you must *write up*—count for 60%. Your writing will consist of roughly seventy-five tightly composed pages of information. This 60% is made up of the following percentage breakdowns:

    16%   Entry 1: Analysis of student writing samples though a series of lessons

    16%   Entry 2: Video and analysis of a full class discussion

    16%   Entry 3: Video and analysis of a small group discussion

    12%   Entry 4: Documented Accomplishments and community participation

The remaining 40% is the *written assessment exam*, which you will schedule and take at your convenience. (See *Chapter 12.*) This 40% is comprised of six questions (6.67% each), which you will answer at an Assessment Center of your choosing. You are allowed 30 minutes per question. Your goal is not to get a perfect score! You need a minimum of 275 'scaled score' points to 'pass'.

The scoring of the portfolio

You have, then, *10 total entries*, which are weighted. All entries are considered as *separate* entries, and are read by different assessors. *The assessors are teachers just like you, teaching in your content area and grade level.*

The rubric against which the entries are measured is valued—and the percentages multiplied—by a number from 4.25 down to 0.75. The higher the number, the more accomplished the work. Here's how the values, or *levels*, break down:

Level 4—Clear, consistent, and convincing evidence is offered. To score at this level, your writing must reflect insightful, logical, in-depth, and appropriate details. Information must be tightly connected and accurately detailed.

Level 3—Similar to the above, but less-detailed, more loosely constructed, and containing information that is more ambiguous. Writing may be clear, but is not as consistent or convincing.

Level 2—Inaccurate or vague information, illogical or too generalized application. A limited amount of *evidence* is offered.

Level 1—Incomplete entries, or entries with unrelated or inappropriate detail. Very unclear, simplistic writing.

Keep in mind—you do not have to score a certain level for any of the entries in order to pass. *It is only your total score that matters.*

It is also important to remember that a different assessor will score each entry of your portfolio. Treat each entry as if it was completely separate in instructional context—it is!

The concern over scoring

One further note. My biggest worry while awaiting my scores was the scoring process. *Don't worry about your entries not being scored 'fairly'.* Now that I understand more about the scoring process, I realize how little I needed to concern myself with that issue! The scoring process is somewhat complicated, but extremely *fair*. There are checks and double checks to be sure no bias, or other scoring issue, enters into your final score. Even a standard deviation (usually between 10–18 points) is figured into the final score to negate any mathematical error. *Bottom line*—if you get your 275 points and pass—you earned it. If you don't, it doesn't make you a poor teacher. Neither does it mean the system was unfair.

Chapter 4

The Standards

(The heart & soul of it all!)

The 'bible' you must write by!

If your box did not contain a hard copy of the *National Standards* in your subject area, order one from *NBPTS*. You need a hard copy to mark up and travel with you. These standards are extrapolated into the *NBPTS Five Core Propositions* referred to in *Chapter 2*. Unless *otherwise portfolio specific*, these standards are the *only* criteria for measurement that will be used by the assessors. Let me repeat that—these standards are the *only* criteria for measurement that will be used by the assessors. It is not necessary for you to address writing standards from your state or your local school district in your portfolio. These *National Standards* are also condensed into the various bulleted instructions in your directions manual. *These standards are the rubric against which your portfolio will be evaluated.*

Survival tidbits checklist regarding the National Standards!

Because the heart and soul of your portfolio is how effectively you *understand, utilize,* and *incorporate* the standards as the backbone of your teaching content, you should consider treating them in the following manner:

❑ Keep the *Standards* book with you often, and read through it *more* often.

❑ Get a highlighter and use it profusely! As you read through the book the first few times, highlight everything that jumps out at you. *Don't be afraid to mark up this book!!!* Among the highlighted items, you might include:

  • *Words* and *phrases* that appear over and over—these are key!

14

- *Concepts* and *ideas* that appear throughout the book.

- Anything the book mentions that *an accomplished teacher* does. Don't miss those verbs!

❑ Next, go through the book a few times with a *red* pen and circle certain 'buzzwords' (See *Chapter 8)* that appear throughout, or words that just sound important. *If they sound important, they probably are!*

❑ Next, as you go through the book in the next few readings, take a *blue* or *green* pen and circle everything mentioned that you *already do* in some form or another. Jot down some quick notes on *how* you do this (evidence) in the wide margins provided.

❑ Finally, using the *Reflections* space at the end of each section, write down how you might put into practice in your classroom these highlighted items from your *Standards* book. That is, how you might put into practice—or put into practice *in a different way*—the concepts, accomplished teacher practices, and exemplars, etc. Write a summary of some of the standards *in your own words* to be sure you understand them.

❑ Treat these standards as if they were the *one and only* criteria against which all the work you are going to do is measured! *They are!* Know them well!

Chapter 5

Waiting for the box!

(Things I can do!)

Congratulations! You have decided to begin the process toward *NBPTS* certification! It will be several weeks before your box arrives. What is this mysterious box? The box is that small, blue and white, perfectly innocuous looking square container that will show up on your doorstep. In it are the forms, the instruction guide, *National Standards* book, and everything else that you will need to propel you toward certification.

Before it arrives, however, there are several things you need to make sure you know in preparation for the journey ahead of you. Many of these things you may have already learned. Others will be new for you. Getting a jump-start on them will make the transition from the world you know, to the world you will experience, much easier!

Learn to use the computer!

You will not have time to learn technology while writing. You will be spending many hours on the computer. You need to be familiar with how the thing works! Find a good word processing program—*Microsoft Word* is the best—and become familiar with such things as the spell-check, auto correct, and auto-insert features. Be sure you know how to paginate, set margins, and insert headers and footers. The most important feature to learn is *auto-save!* This feature will back up your work automatically and has proven a lifesaver to many candidates. Save everything—never assume! This is rule one!

Learn how to use a video camera!

Since you will be making two video entries, start videotaping your classes now for fun. You and your students will get the 'feel' for how to shoot a quality video. Videotaping will be discussed more fully in *Chapter 9*, but you need to be familiar with the basics before you begin. Foremost, be sure you have a good microphone. Purchase one to supplement your video camera if you have to. Become familiar with the technology you will be using to complete the process.

Plan on devoting 110% of your spare time to this process for most of this school year.

The certification process is a time-consuming process. You will need all the support you can get from family and friends. Arrange to have others pick up the load around your home, or get comfortable with the idea of a messy house and 'take-out' meals. Try to limit your family/community commitments during this time. It is important to ask for support from those around you. Much patience and understanding will be required of them.

Research.

If you have been out of the university setting for a number of years, read up on current teaching methodology, strategies, trends, and subject area practices. Become familiar with the legendary *Bloom's Taxonomy*, and *Gardner's Multiple Intelligences*. While you do not have to be an expert in your field to pass the *NBPTS* certification process, you need to be experienced in what works—and doesn't work—in the classroom.

Start hunting!

You can begin compiling one of your four entries even before your box arrives! Start now hunting down and collecting the evidence (known as 'artifacts') you might include in *Entry 4*. Gather all certificates, thank you notes, emails, community projects you were a part of, flyers from workshops, conferences or seminar presentations at which you attended or presented, documentation of university or committee work, and work done with community/parents. Also, include any documentation of collaborative work, parent communiqués, and mentoring logs. Brainstorm how these activities served to increase or enhance student learning and promote student achievement. If they didn't, toss them out.

Start early and save everything.

Start the process as soon as you apply. Even while waiting for your box it helps to start to do some of these things mentioned. Use your time wisely. Start now and save anything that even *might* go in *Entry 4!*

Chapter 6

When the box arrives!

(Here I go—the planning process—
beginning the journey!)

You arrive home and there it is—the box. The *BOX!* In it will be a CD Rom containing standards, instructions, a planner, glossary, and tips. The box will also contain labels and Assessment Center instructions.

The arrival of your box will be a moment you will remember forever. It will rank right up there with your wedding and the birth of your children, and just below the day you mail the thing back! When it comes, you should open it carefully, examine its contents, and find a safe place to put it. You may not want to look at it again till the day you mail it back. There is one thing for certain—you will have a greater reverence for this box in a few months than you could possibly have right now!

Check

First, take all the material out of the box and check to be sure everything is there! Take particular note of the forms you must get signed, mailing labels and envelopes you must keep, and the *National Standards* book. Locate your candidate ID number. This number will become as familiar to you as your birth date!

Organize

Second, organize the material. *Keep everything!* Get a three-ring binder with pockets! Squirrel away all the important 'to be used later' documents in the box itself, and put it in a safe place. However you choose to organize, do so in a way that's simplest for you.

Highlight

Next, get out the portfolio instructions, and find yourself a highlighter. Go through the instructions and *highlight key instructions*—especially the verbs and everything mentioned more than once in the instructions. These are critically important.

Next, find the *National Standards* book if one is included apart from the CD. Skim through it quickly and highlight things that jump out at you. *(See more on this in Chapter 4.)*

Now, put everything away and think about what you've done today. Let some of the highlighted material soak into your brain. Get away from the material and go have a good meal with your family or friends. Discuss with them the excitement of the arrival of the box. There will be time enough to worry about details tomorrow. Enjoy today.

Prioritize

The next day, make a more thorough reading of the portfolio instructions. Highlight anything that jumps out at you that you missed before. Now, read it one more time, and with a red pen, circle key words within your highlighted passages. *Take particular note of bulleted instructions—these are generally condensed versions of the National Standards!* Every word in these instructions is there for a reason! *You will have to answer these completely and accurately, so mark them now.*

Next, do the same thing with the *National Standards* book. Read it through, take notes, and highlight. When you finish, reread it and circle key words.

Schedule

Next, go back to the instructions and find the suggested calendar. Remember, you should mail your box in early March to meet the March 31 deadline. Whatever schedule you develop *it is important to make a flexible calendar.* This is where your scope and sequence comes in! Be sure to include all of your responsibilities—family, community, and professional. Ask yourself how you might reorganize some of your obligations. Decide which entries you want to focus on first. Begin to plan how and when you will proceed. Write idea notes and teaching units on your personal calendar. Start looking ahead. Decide when you will begin additional entries. Recheck your personal calendar often. You may have to adjust the timeline to fit your needs, but at least you will have developed a framework around which to work on your entries. *It is good to plan to finish your basic writing by February 1, and allow five full days to finalize the writing of each entry.*

Copy

Next, gather all the forms you will need to use during the process. These include Verification forms, *(see Chapter 10)*, Contextual Information and Student Release forms, cover sheets for the entries, etc. *Make several copies of everything*, and keep all forms in a separate place. You might want to get an expandable folder for these. Start to get Student Release forms signed and collected. You will be able to do little without these being signed. *You might want to send home with your students a letter of explanation to parents.* Don't forget to get release forms from any adults who might be photographed.

Compartmentalize

Next, decide on how you will organize the four entries of your portfolio. You may want to use four large boxes, or four file folders. If your home is large enough, it wouldn't hurt to use separate rooms! However you choose to organize, divide the entries into four distinct 'units'. The drafts and revisions of your entries will become quite numerous, and you don't want to add confusion to the mix!

Practice

Next, get into the *rhythm of routine*. The rhythm of routine is a mental streamlining of the processes you must go through to reach your goal of *NBPTS* certification. Get into this rhythm by using your parent contact log, continuing to look for artifacts, daily journaling, and taking anecdotal notes of things you might use in the writing. Keep a small notebook to jot things down in. If you will develop the mindset of the *rhythm of routine*, the process will run much smoother.

Establish your work base

Set aside a time and place where you are able to concentrate solely on your *National Board Certification*. Organize so you have quick access to a dictionary, thesaurus, *National Standards* book, the instructions, student papers, lots of paper clips, etc. Make this your base of operations, or 'cubby hole' for the task ahead of you. Arrange for this to be 'off limits' to distractions, interruptions, and your cell phone!

Locate

Finally, locate a support group. (See *Chapter 7*.) Orient family members and friends as to what you are about to undertake. Prepare them for the time and effort you will be required to invest.

Things to remember along the way...

Your knowledge of students is the key to it all!

Your students should be *part* of the process—not merely 'vehicles' to your certification. Your students, more than anything else, are the key to your certification. Get to know them—their interests, their parents, and especially their learning styles. Tell them what you're doing. Include them in the small successes and failures along the way! Let them know you are a learner as well as their teacher, and that this certification process depends a great deal on them. The *NBPTS* wants to see you evidence awareness of your students':

❑ Abilities to relate to real-world experience

❑ Actions, reactions, and the rational for both

❑ Goals and aspirations in life

❑ Growth and development as an individual

❑ Hardships in life and the effect of such

❑ Interests, talents, and learning styles

❑ Interpretive skills regarding issues and events

❑ Peer interaction skills and concerns

❑ Perspective on life and your lessons

❑ Philosophies, values and biases in life

❑ Relationships with adults and their community

❑ Responses to challenges and inquiry

❑ Self-worth and its effect on learning

❑ Socio-economic background and its effect

❑ Special needs in particular areas of learning

Be *sure* you indicate your knowledge of your students throughout your writing!

Decide which students you will feature.

Don't forget that the teaching you feature in *Entries 1–3* must come from different units, different lessons, and different points in time. *You cannot use the same students in dual entries.* Students often react differently when they are being 'featured'. Work with several before you make a final decision. Also consider the time of the year. Especially with younger students, maturity develops later in the year. Remember, you do not have to select your brightest students, but you'd better strongly consider your most dependable and cooperative ones. Consider also, students who are motivated, and may evidence the most improvement through the process

Learn how to scope and sequence.

We all know about scope and sequence in our lessons, don't we? Now, learn to scope and sequence the certification process. That is, learn how to organize the *whole* before you start on the *parts!* Understanding how to look at the 'forest' before analyzing the 'trees' will make the whole certification process easier. You will not be able to start and finish one entry at a time. In fact, don't even *try* to do this. Since you will be jumping between entries, it will help if you keep the purpose and importance of the *whole* process in your mind as you work on each entry. For example, how can you incorporate those *National Standards* in *every* entry—not just one? How can you use those 'buzzwords' (*Chapter 8*) in *all* your writing entries instead of one or two? Doing this helps you develop the understanding of 'what the *NBPTS* is looking for', and through your writing, assures that you consistently presented it.

Don't create a new teacher in the classroom.

This is one of the most important considerations for you to remember. *Do what you already do!* Think about the practices you do with your students that reflect *accomplished teaching*. Show the assessors how good you *already* are! Don't try to be another teacher, or a sterilized clone of what you think the *NBPTS* wants. Just be *you*. You'll find you're probably already doing much of what the *NBPTS* is looking for!

Don't allow yourself to get too stressed out.

During the months you will be working on your portfolio, it will be easy to become so focused that you shut yourself off from everyone and everything. This focus can quickly turn into anxiety and stress. *Stop everything and take a breather once in a while.* Get away from it. Remember to eat well, sleep well, and take time for yourself. Understand that this process will exhaust you. *Budget your time!* Even a few minutes of 'down' time will help alleviate high anxiety levels. Make yourself put the work aside after a certain amount of hours, and a certain amount of days. *It will become all-consuming if you don't.*

Remember to ENJOY the process!

Last, but not least, pace yourself! Along the way, you may feel as though you'll never finish, but you will! Try to enjoy the process! See it for what it really is—*a once in a lifetime opportunity* to hone your craft as a teacher. This is the time to *showcase* your teaching skill and ingenuity! Unfortunately, you may be so busy, so stressed, and so determined to finish, you fail to stop and appreciate the little moments of accomplishment along each step of the way. *Celebrate these accomplishments!* Each one leads to the day you mail in that box!

Chapter 7

Outside help

(I am not alone...)

Although you are going to find this certification process to be lonely at times, never forget that throughout the process, you are never alone. There is an abundance of outside help to assist you.

Networking

Access the *NBPTS* site and listserv contacts as soon as you apply for the certification process. There are no penalties for seeking help. The Internet resources help to familiarize you with the process and allow you to be in contact with current candidates and mentors in your subject area.

Locate and contact other current, past and/or future candidates via email or district help groups. Keep in touch! *Networking is a lifesaver!*

Mentors

Don't be afraid to ask for help! Seek out a mentor. Even if the mentor is from another subject area, it's OK. There will be times when you just need an ear to listen and advise. Some states offer not only mentors, but also mentoring support (cohort) groups that meet on a regular basis. Mentors within these groups work with candidates in various certification areas. *Taking advantage of this opportunity is the one single most important thing you can do.*

Chat rooms and message boards

OK, this one is controversial. Many will disagree, but I suggest you locate and utilize the online chat and support groups such as the ones in *YAHOO* geared to *NBPTS* certification. Many are listed here. These support groups are made up of individuals who are willing to help you at virtually any time of the day or night. These individuals do not have to be in your subject area. *Often, it is to your benefit if they are not.* They can sometimes lend a different perspective to your work. (Remember however, you alone are responsible to know the correct make up of your portfolio!) They offer the experience of teachers who have passed their board certification, as well as those who have yet to pass. The insights and suggestions available in these online resources are invaluable. Remember, however, these individuals are constrained by *NBPTS* policy on how specific they can be in helping you. For example, they cannot tell you Assessment Center questions, or be too specific regarding how you should compose your writing portfolio. *Utilize their assistance, but don't put them on the spot.*

Contact NBPTS by phone: *1-800-22TEACH*

Helpful websites

These are all a part of the official *National Board* website.

Site Map
http://www.NBPTS.org/sitemap/index.html

Candidate Resource Center
http://www.NBPTS.org/candidates/index.cfm

NBPTS Candidate Guide
http://www.nbpts.org/candidates/guide/:

Discussion Groups
http://www.NBPTS.org/events/discus.cfm

NBPTS Standards
http://www.nbpts.org/standards/index.cfm

NBPTS scoring guides
http://www.NBPTS.org/candidates/scoringguides.cfm

Candidate Inquiry Service
https://nbpts4.ets.org/cis/

Contact NBPTS
http://www.NBPTS.org/help/index.cfm

Assessment Center help
http://www.nbpts.org/candidates/acob/4_preptstdy.html

Here are some *additional* websites:

Yahoo chat rooms regarding the *NBPTS*
http://groups.yahoo.com/

Join *NBPTS* discussion groups under specific areas of certification. Done in message board format, this is one of the most helpful sites around! Former candidates provide an invaluable source of help (and encouragement!) at virtually any hour! *Bookmark this one!*

Teachers.net
http://www.teachers.net/

Teachers.net offers live chat forums and message board discussions. On a message board, you can post questions and receive answers from others who have already received their certification from the *NBPTS*.

***NBPTS* trials and triumphs!**
http://groups.yahoo.com/group/nationalboardquest/

This is another of the many information centers regarding the *NBPTS*.

Chapter 8

The Writing Process!

(The essence of everything!)

Your writing is the heart and soul of your portfolio. It is the essence of what you are sending the assessors. If you do not write reasonably well, you're in trouble. The evidence you write about must follow the infamous 'C' words that you will hear until you are sick of them. You must write:

❑ Crisply—short, to the point sentences.

❑ Clearly—explain everything and never assume.

❑ Correctly—proper grammar goes without saying.

❑ Concisely—get to the point and move on.

❑ Convincingly—build a wall of evidence.

Choosing the lesson

Since you will be writing four entries—three involving students—you will need to spend some time deciding which lessons you want to use. Do not assume that your best lesson to *teach* is necessarily your best lesson to *use*. Remember—*'tried and true may not be best to do!'* Ask yourself the following questions to help you decide which lesson to use:

❑ Which lesson will benefit and *evidence* student learning across a *range* of content?

❑ Which lesson will *challenge* my students across a range of disciplines?

❑ Which lesson will best evidence *me as a learner?*

❏ Which lesson will best address the *National Standards*?

❏ Which lesson might be so familiar that my reflection and analysis could be stunted?

Choosing the students

While you are limited in the number of classes you may choose from in your two videotaped entries, you may choose from *all* of your students in *Entry 1*. *Know your students!* Individual interests, beliefs, attitudes, values, experiences and skills—they bring all of these to you! Remember, you do not have to select your brightest students. *Dependability* and *cooperation* should be a guiding influence in your selection process. In selecting students to feature in *Entry 1*, consider which students will be more likely to exhibit the most *improvement*.

Preparing to write

❏ Find a good word processing program. *Microsoft Word* is the best. Be sure you know how to paginate, use *auto-text* and *auto-correct* features, set margins, and insert headers and footers. The most important feature to remember is *auto-save!* Set it to 'one minute' and save everything—*never assume!*

❏ Learn to use:

- *Auto insert*

- *Auto correct* (as you type)

- *Spell check* (formal, standard, and casual)

- *Find and Replace*

- *Grammar statistics/reading level*

❏ Use *only 12 point Times Roman* font. Don't forget to double-space, set margins, paginate, etc. Use only one side of each page.

❏ Create mailing label stickers with your candidate ID number on each one. Make sure to put these in the *top right* corner of every page.

❏ Try to break up the text every once and awhile. Long, flowing narrative is a strain to read. *Paragraph often.*

❏ Be careful about your use of student names! Use initials or first names only. Don't forget to white-out last names. *Preserve anonymity.*

❏ Don't use your own name in the written commentary—even when quoting a student.

Understand the terms! The types of writing the NBPTS expects

You must distinguish between three types of writing when composing your written work. One of the leading causes of reduced scoring in the *NBPTS* certification process is a failure to distinguish between these three types of writing, and failing to *fully* address the requirements listed in each type.

In the course of your writing, you will be asked to write in three style formats. Be sure you can recognize and perform each type.

Descriptive writing

Descriptive writing creates a picture. It simply *describes, lists*, or *summarizes*. It *sets the scene*, and answers *what, when, where*, and *how*. Descriptive writing provides *basic information*, and *background*. In your descriptive writing, address the following mental questions:

• What are the *goals* of the lesson?

• How did you *assess* whether the goals were met?

• How did you adapt for student *diversity*?

• How did the assignment *connect* to other activities?

• What are the key *concepts* in the lesson?

• What is the logical *order* of the lesson?

• What happened *prior* to the lesson?

• What does the assessor need to know about your students?

• What *resources* did you use and why?

• How does the lesson *impact student learning*?

- How did the students *respond*?

- Were student responses *accurate*?

- What type of student *feedback* did I give?

Analytical writing

The *'Hemmingway Iceberg Theory'* of writing states that 15% is descriptive, while 85% should be analytical. Analytical or *interpretive* writing involves breaking down, examining, and explaining information. It furnishes *reasons* and *motives*, and demonstrates *significance*. Analytical writing answers the *what's* of descriptive writing with *why's*, *how's*, and *so what's* regarding your teaching strategies, and your lesson's goals, objectives, and effectiveness. Simply stated, analytical writing allows for the *'what it all means'* regarding your lesson, as well as how your students understand the lesson. Keep in mind too, selecting a few direct quotes from your videos can enhance the analytical aspect of your writing! Analytical phrasing might include phrasing such as:

> "Student results indicated…"
> "This activity promoted…"
> "I did this because…"

In your analytical writing, address the following mental questions:

- What did the lesson tell you about your students?

- What feedback strategies did you use to promote learning? Why these?

- How did your feedback help change or reinforce student learning?

- What did your students learn through this lesson? How do you *know*? (Don't forget to cite examples!)

- What did you hope to accomplish in this lesson?

- What is the significance of this lesson?

- What were some *inconsistencies* in the lesson?

- How did the lesson relate to the needs of your students?

- What happened as a result of this lesson?

- What aspects of the lesson *need improvement?*

- Why did you choose to use the resources you did?

Reflective writing

Reflective writing is your mirror. It is your bridge to the future, where you 'bear your soul' citing what you did right and wrong, and tell what you would do next time. Reflective writing answers the questions: 'What did *you learn* from the lesson and student work?' 'What would you *modify* or *do differently* if you were to do the lesson again?' Include both the positives and negatives. *Reflective writing is not a summary, or conclusion!* It is *self-analysis.* It is simply a personal look-back on the lesson, and how you could make it better if you were doing it again! *Remember, reflection emphasizes improvement—it isn't a forum for explaining a lack of perfection!*

Reflective phrasing might include phrasing such as:

> "This helped me realize…"
> "I became more aware…"
> "My intent in doing this was…"

In your reflective writing, address the following mental questions:

- What part of your planning/teaching regarding this lesson would you do *differently* next time?

- How will changes benefit student learning? How do you know?

- What short and long-term *goals* should you set for your students based upon your assessment of their performance regarding this lesson?

- What did you learn about yourself as a teacher?

- What did you learn *from* your students?

- In what areas do you need to improve as a teacher? Why these?

- Why did some students respond as they did?

- Based upon your analysis, how might you alter your feedback strategies?

- What did you learn about your preparation?

- What did you learn about student readiness?

- What patterns or trends did you see that emerged?

And now, let the writing begin!

❑ Remember your audience! *The assessor is a teacher just like you!* Do not attempt to impress them by your writing. Your writing is an *explanation*, not a dissertation!

❑ Keep in mind that your written commentary is the final visible result of all your labor! *How you write about what you did is the most important key to a successful portfolio!*

❑ As an attorney builds a case, carefully compile your evidence!

❑ As you write, talk *to* the reader—not *at* the reader! *Be yourself!*

❑ If writing exemplars are provided in the instructions, read through these three or four times noting *why* these are exemplars.

❑ Use *your* voice! The more your writing reflects your style and voice, the easier it will be to appreciate! Do not try to be someone else in your writing.

❑ Include rubrics in *Entry 1*. (Student-generated rubrics are especially strong pieces.)

❑ Limit bolding and underlining. A little goes a long way.

❑ Circle key words! Note sentence structure! *When you finish, write down seven things that made each an exemplar.*

❑ As you type, back up at regular intervals. Make sure you save, save, *save!*

❑ Copy *everything*. Make a duplicate copy of your portfolio as it is completed. You will not get your portfolio back when the process is over.

❑ If you are using auto save, set it to save *every minute*. Save a copy on a disk or CD just in case!

❑ Be sure to keep your *tenses* the same!

❑ Discuss *negatives* (student non-participation, things you forgot, failed to address, could have included, etc.) as well as the positives in your lesson. Remember—even the things that went wrong can be analyzed as long as you point out *what you might do differently next time*. Do not discount the value of lessons *you* learned from the experience! Remember too—it's your *practice*—not the *success* of your lesson—that's important.

❑ Remember your page limitations. Assessors will stop reading at those limits.

❑ *Take particular note of bulleted instructions in the portfolio instructions!* You've already highlighted and circled these. Be sure you answer these precisely and completely! These are generally condensed versions (core values) of the *National Standards!* It is against these standards alone that your work will be measured! *Every word in these instructions is there for a reason!*

❑ Copy and tape the bulleted core values to your monitor!

❑ When writing the commentary on your videos, refer to *all* students, and gear everything to *impact on student learning*.

❑ Be sure your writing reflects what's on the tape! Don't forget to explain the *setting*, prior learning or previous lesson, and your *objectives* or *goals* for this entry.

❑ Someone not in your subject area should read your final drafts.

❑ As you are writing, be sure you are listing *clear, consistent, convincing, concrete* evidence! Ask yourself *'so what?'* Be sure your presented evidence:

  • Impacts student accomplishment

  • Evidences student improvement

  • Relates to the impact of your teaching

  • Reflects the *National Standards*

❑ Don't assume anything—think like the reader, explain everything you can, and use the handy *'for example'* when you want to be sure the assessor gets it. Always emphasize *why!*

❑ Don't abbreviate unless you are absolutely certain the assessors will know what it means! *Avoid acronyms.*

❑ Remember—*space is at a premium*. Don't repeat yourself for emphasis. State your point clearly, then move on. *Repetition will not make your writing better. It only makes it redundant!*

❑ Brevity is the key! Keep your sentences *short & lean!* Cut the fluff! Elaborate in your *teaching*—cut to the chase in your *writing*. Don't make the assessor have to read between the lines to find your point! If it's not obvious, it's not right.

❑ Remember—it is *your practice*—not the *students' achievement level* that counts!

❑ Insert examples of the *National Standards* you are addressing in parenthesis each time you cite one in the text. You can put each standard and number into your *auto insert* function. While the assessors are required to recognize each time you address a standard, it doesn't hurt to make sure! *(Don't over do this. A few will go a long way.)*

❑ Make constructive comments (feedback) on student work in *Entry 1* which evidences you understand any difficulty students might be having. *Compliment progress.*

❑ Unless you are asked to do so, don't throw in a litany of researchers and their theories.

❑ Whenever possible *show* rather than *tell.* Evidence is stronger than concepts. For example, instead of saying "I valued student choice and inquiry," *describe* how the lesson gave students choices and opportunities for inquiry.

❑ Use the *active*—not *passive*—voice in your writing. It's easier to read, more powerful, and saves space!

❑ Restate the prompt to be sure you answered it completely.

❑ *Streamline and focus!* Keep your analytical writing in a 'flow pattern' based upon student needs. Your pattern should flow something like this: *student need* contributes to the *lesson goals. Lesson goals* are evaluated through *assessment. Assessment* determines *student needs,* etc.

❑ Be consistent throughout your writing. (Hyphenation, font, comma use, italics, use of bold and underline, etc.)

Use the language! (Buzzwords)

It is important that you speak the language of the *National Standards* in your writing. It is more important that you use your own voice in the process! If you choose to incorporate some of the so-called buzzwords listed below, remember that overuse results in stiff, stilted, and ineffective writing. *Do not sacrifice your voice at the expense of overusing buzzwords!*

- *above and beyond the average teacher*
- *active engagement*
- *advance student understanding*
- *application based*
- *applicational thinking*
- *appropriate assessment*
- *assessment based*
- *behavior intervention*
- *beyond the classroom*
- *broad and comprehensive understanding*
- *challenging*
- *clear, convincing, connecting, consistent*
- *community involvement*
- *connections to the real world*
- *conscious and deliberate*
- *constructive feedback*
- *content oriented*
- *critical thinking*
- *cross curricular*
- *decision-making skills*
- *demonstrated*
- *direct impact on student learning*
- *directly relevant*
- *diverse perspective*
- *dynamic interactions*
- *effectively manage*
- *empower students*
- *encourage*
- *engaging*
- *equality & diversity*
- *equitable*
- *evidenced*
- *facilitation of learning*
- *fairness*
- *for example*
- *goal related*

- *high expectation*
- *How do I know? I know because…*
- *I learned*
- *I should have*
- *inclusiveness*
- *increased student learning*
- *insightful questions*
- *instructional goals*
- *integrated classroom*
- *interdisciplinary*
- *inviting classroom*
- *learning centered*
- *learning community*
- *learning goals*
- *meaningful*
- *measurable increase in student learning*
- *measured improvement*
- *meets standards*
- *modeling*
- *motivational*
- *next time*
- *non threatening*
- *now I understand*
- *on task*
- *outcome based*
- *parent partnership*
- *peer to peer encouragement*
- *problem solving*
- *productive classroom*
- *professional growth*
- *promote highest achievement*
- *real-world relevance*
- *reflect incisively*
- *relevant characteristics*
- *reluctant learner*
- *rich and in-depth*

- *rich variety of sources*
- *risk-taking*
- *safe and welcoming environment*
- *standards based*
- *stimulating variety*
- *student centered*
- *student empowerment*
- *student interchange*
- *student learning*
- *student ownership*
- *student perspective*
- *students as individual learners*
- *substantive teaching*
- *supportive*
- *teacher as learner*
- *teacher-directed*
- *teaching strategies*
- *technology enhanced*
- *this shows*
- *two-way interaction & communication*
- *unique learning needs*
- *value diversity*
- *varied assessment*
- *work collaboratively*

Final writing tips 'n tidbits checklist!

❑ Include at least one Verification form, (though *only* one is probably enough). *Your Verification form is used to validate an accomplishment for which you may have no tangible artifact. (See Chapter 10.)*

❑ Make sure your pages are *legible* and *numbered.*

❑ Once you start writing your entries, find readers—friends, family, and colleagues—to read your drafts. Even if you ask a non-teacher, it will help to check for the clarity of writing.

❑ *(Continue to seek support. You will be getting very tired. Contact mentors or support groups for emotional support, as well as for updates on National Board process inquiries.)*

❑ As you complete entries, let them 'rest' for a few days. Reread them after you have taken a break from them. They may appear differently to fresh eyes!

❑ Before you complete your writing, be sure you *addressed the prompts, subheadings, and bulleted instructions clearly, accurately, and completely!* These reflect the *National Standards*, and your primary job throughout is to *demonstrate how your teaching reflects the concepts of these standards!*

❑ Be sure you did exactly what the instructions asked you to do! Write *to* the question—not *about* the question! *Probe what they're asking!*

Ask yourself the following questions as you finish the writing process for your entries:

• Was the lesson goal *clear and obvious*?

• Did the assignment *demonstrate the learning goals?*

• Did students *understand the concepts* taught?

• Did I *address misunderstandings?*

• Did I *discuss rubrics* used in assessments?

• Was there some evidence of *assessment by students?*

• Did I give *constructive feedback?*

• What do I *need to reteach* about the lesson?

Chapter 9

Taping!

(Getting it right!)

You will be taping *Entries 2 and 3* of your portfolio. In these entries, more than any of the others, *Murphy's Law* will prove to be true! Be prepared! In dealing with technology, anything that *can* go wrong *will* go wrong!

Remember that the tapes are merely the vehicles for what really counts—your writing. Writing is the key!

What the NBPTS wants to see—considerations regarding your best videotape

- How your knowledge *deepens the thinking* of your students.

- How well you can link your teaching topic to *present application.*

- How well you integrate *technology.*

- How well you *actively engage* all your students.

- How well you *set high expectations* and goal-oriented learning.

- How well you *address diversity* and foster respect.

- How well your students can *reason, discuss,* and *conclude.*

The focus of your taped entries

The main focus of your taped entries is to show the assessors:

- the atmosphere and *learning climate* you create for your students

- that you are able to facilitate, as well as motivate students to work alone and in groups

- the *essence* of what you want assessors to appreciate and understand as they view your tapes

- that you are addressing the *National Standards*

- that you handled the *anticipated,* the *expected,* and the *unexpected* incidents

- the on-task *engagement* of your students in their learning process, how you responded, and what *you* learned about off-task behaviors

- the *interaction* (verbal and nonverbal) between students, and teacher/students in the learning process

- the discourse and *relevance* of your lesson, and how it helped students achieve instructional goals

Key things to remember about taped entries

❑ Be sure you have release forms from all students and adults to be taped.

❑ Be sure you do not use the same students in both taping entries. There must be no overlap of students or lessons.

❑ Make simple videos to get your students and yourself familiar with the taping process. The more familiar your students become with the process, the less difficulty you will have with 'kids being kids' when the camera is on.

❑ Label each tape with the *entry number, date,* and a brief *comment.* Make a duplicate copy—just in case.

❑ Get over the initial shock of seeing yourself on camera. *Yes, you really do sound like that, but you also look a whole lot better!* If you might need technical assistance with equipment, arrange for this early. Check your test videos for clear picture and sound. *Eliminate surprises!*

❑ Learn to ignore the camera, and teach your students to do the same.

❑ Remember, your setting does not have to be in the classroom, but one of the entries probably should be.

❑ Keep in mind, if you select direct quotes from your videos can help in the 'analysis' aspect of your writing.

❑ Be sure to prepare your room so that the least amount of distraction will occur. Consider closing windows and shades, turning off the phone, and notifying others that this is 'taping day'. Put a note on your door.

❑ Consider the best placement for your camera and microphone. Get a *long* extension cord just in case.

❑ Be sure any board work or artifacts you are using are easily seen in the video.

❑ Check the battery in the camera. Keep a spare on hand just in case.

❑ Tape in the *highest quality* mode possible!

❑ Make sure you have enough light.

❑ Don't forget to include your classroom layout when packing this entry.

❑ You might consider investing in a supplementary *Pressure Zone Microphone* (PZM), which you may want to hang from the ceiling. This microphone inhibits background noise. Often, student voices cannot be heard distinctly when using built-in microphones that come with the camera. While scorers generally have equipment that allows them to amplify sound as they view your tape, it won't hurt to 'assist' them as you record.

❑ If you find you just filmed the 'perfect' video, but the students' voices are too low to hear clearly, remember—you can always script the inaudible parts. (Scripting does take up an inordinate amount of space however, and in your writing, every inch of your permitted pages should be utilized.)

❑ If you are considering using a tripod to ensure a sharp, clear video, keep in mind that a stationary camera yields the *poorest* sound. Since it is important to include *all* your students, you might consider letting someone walk around with the camera when you film. Students generally work much better as videographers than do adults. Having a student run the camera creates a more comfortable class environment, and a relaxed environment is the key to successful classroom taping!

❑ Share your videos with a colleague or friend. Get their input on what worked and what *didn't*. Be sure you are meeting the requirements expected in each entry. Also, be sure it is *obvious* that you're meeting them. Never assume. Leave nothing to speculation. Make sure you are furnishing clear, convincing evidence for meeting the requirements of the entry Incorporate the buzz-words, but do so *sparingly!*

❑ Remember the editing rules. You must submit an *unedited* and *continuous* section. Only the first 15 minutes will be evaluated. If the tape stops, it's done, so be careful.

❑ If you are using the older style videotapes, punch out the tab in the casing so it is impossible to tape over it! *Remember Murphy's Law!!!*

❑ In your group video, remember—the session is only as good as the member in it who is contributing the *least*. The key is 'active engagement'. Make sure everyone has a job, and is participating.

❑ When you have narrowed your best videos down to two or three, watch each one *four* times.

➢ Watch it once *by yourself.* Take notes on the positives and negatives of the session.

➢ Watch it once *with your students.* Note any insightful comments they may make, and include these in your writing analysis and reflection.

➢ Watch it once *with a friend or colleague.* Solicit their input.

➢ Watch it once *silently.* Analyze and reflect in your writing what your session tells you from the four viewings.

Tips 'n tidbits checklist for the analysis and reflection of your tape

When analyzing and reflecting on your tape, consider the following questions:

❑ Could all my students' *faces be seen?*

❑ Were all *my students engaged* or involved to some degree?

❑ Did I encourage reluctant learners and discuss this in my writing?

❑ Did I *restate* and *clarify* when necessary?

❑ Was *risk-taking promoted,* so that my students felt comfortable?

❑ What *shows* the success or failure of my lesson?

❑ Is there a *better class* I could've chosen for this lesson?

❑ What evidence reveals *students were* learning?

❑ Were the students achieving my lesson's objectives?

❑ Have I demonstrated to the assessor that the students achieved the lesson's objectives?

❑ What and how would I *change something* in this lesson?

❑ Are the students coming to their own conclusions?

❑ Did I address the special needs, interests, and *multiple intelligences* of my students?

❑ Are the *students seeing relevance* in the lesson?

❑ Was the lesson age-appropriate?

❑ Is it obvious to the assessor that the lesson was age-appropriate?

❑ Could everyone (including me) be heard sufficiently?

❑ Was there evidence of student decision-making skills?

❑ Did I allow 'wait time' after my questioning?

❑ Were the *National Standards* reflected in this lesson?

❑ How did I handle any 'teachable moments'?

❑ Could I have arranged the students differently?

❑ Did I redirect my students appropriately when necessary?

❑ Does the lesson *reflect diversity* within my classroom?

❑ What does the body language of my students say?

❑ Did I challenge students through *higher-level questions?*

❑ Were all necessary artifacts seen clearly?

❑ Did I give *appropriate feedback* to answered questions?

❑ Did I prepare the students sufficiently for learning in this lesson?

❑ Were the *students connecting the lesson* to any prior learning?

❑ Did I address any *misconceptions* appropriately?

❑ Did I handle unexpected interruptions appropriately?

❑ What does the *student interaction* tell me about this lesson?

❑ Did I show evidence of my ability to pose meaningful work?

❑ Did the videos reflect *student understanding?*

❑ Did the videos reflect *constructive feedback?*

Chapter 10

Entry #4

(So, what exactly is a 'documented accomplishment?')

What is a *documented accomplishment?* Is it an accolade? Is it a "Teacher of the Year" award you may have won? Is a documented accomplishment an article you wrote for a journal, or can it simply be something you do on a regular basis at your school?

To the *NBPTS*, a documented accomplishment is some particular evidence of:

- you as a *continual learner*—professional growth
- you as a *leader/collaborator*—regarding your peers and colleagues within the *last five* years
- *you as partner*—reaching out to families and community within the *current* school year

While you may be stronger in one particular category, you should *include evidence from all three*. You must provide evidence in at least one of these categories for each documented accomplishment.

You must connect your accomplishment to student learning or the *likelihood* of student learning.

It is also important to *balance* the number of artifacts you include with the number of pages you are allowed to write. *Remember, balance is the key; student learning is the essence!*

Preparing to document accomplishments

Start early and save everything from the last five years. (*See Chapter 5.*)

The qualification for a documented accomplishment

Analyze how you collaborate with other teachers and administrators. Get in the habit of documenting these types of events and situations. Remember, to qualify, the accomplishment must exhibit an *intentional, conscious and deliberate focus* on improving teaching and learning, as opposed to merely fulfilling a job requirement. After school, extra-school, or beyond the classroom activities are the good rules of thumb. If it is something expected of every teacher, it probably doesn't qualify as a documented accomplishment. The accomplishment must be *beyond the routine*.

The process of documenting an accomplishment

Some candidates suggested doing *Entry 4* first. Some say they preferred doing it last. My best advice is to start this one first and finish it last. In fact, always go back through all your entries *many times* before you send the box. You don't have to redo all of them—just revisit them. After you've been away from them awhile, you will see them with fresh eyes. When you have selected your entries, remember that *quality* is more important than quantity. Choose only enough documented accomplishments that you can adequately analyze and reflect upon. Assessors will be looking for *clear, consistent, and convincing* evidence of student learning (or the *likelihood* of student learning) in your writing. *Remember, all the assessors have is what you tell them.* Include:

- Why this accomplishment is important to you, your students, your school, community, etc.

- How the *National Standards* are addressed.

- What positive changes and/or improvements the accomplishment created in your teaching practices and classroom.

Cautions about documenting accomplishments

Keep your *personal accomplishments* discussion to a minimum. *'Teacher of the Year' accolades are not usually your best choices for entries.* In addition, some entries may overlap. That is, they may evidence you as a learner and a collaborator, or involve parents as a part of the community. If you use dual entries, be sure you explain the particular *focus*. The questions below include the most important things you need to remember about each entry you are considering including as an 'accomplishment':

✓ Why is this *important?*

✓ What impact did this have *on my students?*

✓ What impact did this have *on student learning?*

✓ *How do I know* this was successful in impacting my students' learning?

✓ Is this something *above and beyond* what would be expected of every teacher, or is it one that is *routine* and *required?*

✓ Does this accomplishment reflect how I *recognized* and *met* a student need? (It is important that you *meet* student needs—not just recognize them!)

✓ Was this accomplishment *during the last five years?* (Note that some entries require evidence from the *current* school year!)

✓ Do my accomplishments *reflect the National Standards?*

Tips 'n tidbits checklist for documenting an accomplishment

What are some things you might consider including as artifacts for this entry? Accomplishments could include:

❑ a signed agenda book

❑ a student monitoring contract

❑ online, teacher-created web pages (such as *Schoolnotes.com*) to keep students and parents continually informed, or a web page of student helps

❑ a communication log—a *series* of parent contacts through phone logs, and/or emails regarding a particular student *(two-way communication is the key!)*

❑ a newspaper article about you with quotes from former students

❑ peer coaching contracts

❑ online student reviews (of books or films) that evidence student accomplishment (*Amazon.com* welcomes these)

❑ student work denoting use of a new skill

❑ a copy of improved state test scores in your area

❑ at least one Verification form (Your Verification form is used to validate an accomplishment—*and* its impact on student learning—for which you may have no tangible artifact.) *Be sure what is written on the Verification form matches what you explain in your entry, and that the person verifying states clearly how they the accomplishment impacted student learning.*

❑ parent letters extolling a learning strategy that was especially successful.

❑ a letter from an esteemed colleague or notable educator or community person

❑ letters or articles you wrote for professional journals

❑ a personal, reflective journal

❑ having community-based, non-profit organizations (such as Junior Achievement, Rotary Clubs, etc.) come and work with your students for an extended period.

❑ leadership roles in professional organizations

❑ student-led conferences where students help students by sharing achievement strategies

❑ community photos (Don't tape them in—*scan* them in. Appearance counts!)

❑ documented evidence of your attendance or presentation at a conference or workshop

❑ newsletters

❑ parent surveys and questionnaires

❑ especially poignant student letters

❑ mentoring or student teaching assignments

Whatever you include, make sure that your evidence is *clear, concrete, convincing and continual,* and that it resulted in—or was likely to result in—student learning. Never forget—*student learning* is the key! (**NOTE:** Student learning, in the broadest sense of the word, could be a result of improvements in cognitive, social, behavioral, therapeutic, or emotional skills.) If you can't tie it in to this, don't use it as an entry.

Chapter 11

Packing the box!

(When the portfolio is finished—sending it in!)

Once you have everything completed, it's time to send your box home. *You should plan to mail your box at least two weeks prior to the due date.*

You probably feel you've left something incomplete. Realize that the entries are never finished, they're just 'done', and you have to mail them. *Perfection isn't achievable*, neither is it the goal.

Ask yourself these questions as you tie everything together:

❑ Did I follow the *NBPTS* rules about student names, my ID number, fonts, margins, pagination, etc.?

❑ Did I spellcheck everything *several* times?

❑ Did I include my classroom layout?

❑ Did I include all required forms including attestation, Contextual Information and Candidate Final Inventory sheets? Remember—you do not have to submit Adult and Student Release forms, but you must get them signed anyway.

❑ Did I make the appropriate distinction in my writing between the terms: *analyze, describe, & reflect?*

❑ Did I make sure my *ID number*, date, and *signature* is on everything it should be?

❑ Did I punch out the tabs on my videotapes, rewind them, and put the *correct* label?

❑ Did I check the Candidate Final Inventory for each entry?

❑ Did I check student work samples against the description in my written commentary to make sure I referred to the correct student?

❑ Did I omit last names and school locale references?

❑ Did I put my candidate ID bar code on each entry coversheet, envelope, and on the portfolio box?

❑ Did I make final copies of everything—student work, videotapes, computer disks, entries, etc.? (Make a duplicate copy of your portfolio as it is completed. You do not get your portfolio back when the process is over.)

Get your 'box' out of storage. Review packing directions *before* you start packing. Allow for a few days to pack the box.

Start packing your box. *Make sure you follow all directions.* You do not need to send in your Student Release forms. You just sign the form that says you have them. Store the Student Release forms in a safe place for future reference, if needed.

Gather your Verification forms *(see Chapter 10)*. Be sure you have included at least one from a principal or administrator.

Have someone check your packed box.

Mail it!

Celebrate the *completion* of the process—you can celebrate passing later.

Here's a quick reference guide I give to my candidates as they are winding up their writing. It's an acronym entitled *'The Home Stretch'*:

T—tenses should be correct. Tenses don't do well in mixed company.
H—have all my forms completed (class layout, release forms, etc.)
E—engaged students in my videos! If not, tell why!

H—high expectations evidenced in my videos—clearly observable.
O—only active voice in the majority of my writing. Write the way you speak.
M—make copies of everything before sending anything!
E—examples cited for generalizations! "For example" is your best assurance of evidence.

S—standards-based vocabulary. Use the language by which you're scored!

T—tightly written narrative. Streamline! Say it and move on.

R—relevant lesson connections. Real-world is a must.

E—evidence of student learning presented clearly, consistently and convincingly.

T—technically correct margins, font, spelling, ID #'s, etc.

C—completely address every question, prompt, etc. Answer what you're asked!

H—have at least two educators and one non-educator read every entry.

Chapter 12

The Assessment Center

(Your final exam!)

While you may take the assessment exam *before* or *after* your complete your portfolio, it is generally recommended that you take the exam last.

What's it all about?

The written assessment exam, which you will take at an Assessment Center of your choosing, counts 40% of your total score. The 40% is comprised of six questions (6.67% each). You are allowed 30 minutes per question.

To study or not to study...

It really is true—you need not concern yourself with laborious study for the Assessment Center exam. *You'll either know it or you won't.* This is not to say you shouldn't brush up on your subject matter. There are dozens of helpful study guides available. Utilize them. Nevertheless, the questions are created to test the *general knowledge* of your subject. To over-study for the assessment exam may produce diminishing returns.

The preparation process

Make your appointment 30 days in advance at one of the over 300 Assessment Centers. Also, check a month before the exam to be sure you're aware of what areas for testing will be addressed.

If possible, go to an 'Assessment Center practice' website. In the past, there have been a number of such websites available. You cannot take the test, but you can become familiar with the testing environment and procedure. If you have taken a test on a computer before (like the GRE), you'll be fine. It's the same format. Study a level 4 rubric to see exactly what they will be looking for.

Review the *Assessment Center Booklet*. Make note of the time frame for your subject area assessment, and review the subject area suggestions in the booklet. Review literature, teaching materials, and websites, which may relate to the assessment.

Also, be sure to eat right, sleep, and exercise in the days before the test. The goal is to reduce the stress involved with test taking, however you choose to do this. Get a good night's sleep the night before, and a good breakfast the day of.

When you get there

When you get to the Assessment Center, try to locate a computer far away from others who may be there. This gives you privacy, and every advantage helps. When testing begins, work as rapidly as you are able. If you are given a question about which you don't have a clue, *write something*. If you can think of nothing else, tie the subject matter to *student learning, National Standards,* and *student achievement.* These are your 'aces in the hole' when your mind draws a blank! Do not concern yourself about what the scorer might think when they read your attempt at the answer. You will never meet the scorer—just do your best.

On test day, don't try to go out for lunch. You don't need the stress. Use your breaks to meditate, chill out, and refresh. It's a long day!

Also, bring along some high carb, lo-fat snacks. These will help keep your thought processes functioning!

The assessment center exercises are not writing ability assessments. You may answer using connected paragraphs, or choose to answer some questions using a bulleted list. What matters are specific and detailed responses to the questions asked. It is important to read the questions or prompts carefully and direct your answers specifically to what the prompts ask. Detail and clarity are valued in high-scoring responses.

Assessment Center tips 'n tidbits

✓ Use the clock (which you have the choice of hiding) on the computer screen.

✓ Arrive about 30 minutes early to become acclimated.

✓ Remember to take your *Authorization to Test* (ATT) verification, two valid forms of identification, and your sheet of bar code labels.

✓ Make sure your key ideas are cited before you worry about appearances and details.

✓ Hit the *National Standards*, student achievement, and real-world application.

✓ Include what you already know, and address possible misconceptions.

✓ Relate your discussion to broad generalities—the 'big picture' aspect.

✓ Write *clearly* and *concisely!* You will be evaluated on your content, not your fluency. If time permits, you should clean up your sentence and paragraph structure.

✓ Be sure you read and answer the question *carefully* and *completely*, and that you answer *all parts* of the question! To leave out any part is to suffer a substantial reduction in score!

✓ Skip introductions and conclusions. *Get* to the point, *maximize* the point and *move on.*

✓ Include any factual and or statistical detail *you know to be true and accurate.* Numbers and facts lend an air of authority to your writing.

✓ Formulate and utilize *cause and effect* information where you are able. This exemplifies higher-level reasoning skills.

✓ Cite *examples* where you are able. Illustrated evidence is *strong* evidence.

✓ Be dogmatic in your opinions. Do not say, *"I think"*, or *"it is possible."* These weaken your discussion.

Chapter 13

The wait for your scores!

(When it's all over & done, what if...?)

The last farewell

The box has finally been mailed. The Assessment Center exam—*done!* You are feeling relief that you have typed your last word. You are feeling apprehension that perhaps you did not pack your box correctly. When you have finished the process, be sure you understand what an accomplishment this really was! You will have just contributed several months out of your life, not to mention funds from your bank account! You should feel very, very proud of what you've done! The only thing left now is to wait for the scores and see if you passed. Statistics say you have a 40% chance of passing the first time around. Relax; your scores won't be available for 6–9 months.

The scores are posted...

I recall speaking at the *NMSA* Conference in 2002 during the period when the scores were about to be released. I remember hearing the buzz among conference attendees: "the scores have been posted online!" I will never forget rushing to the nearest computer, and logging on to the *NBPTS* website. Nor will I forget watching another candidate leave the room in tears as I was walking in. As I logged on to the site, my heart was in my throat. Would all the work be for naught? Would the scorers not appreciate my effort? My eyes closed as the message regarding my score flashed on the screen. At last, I finally got up the nerve to peek at the screen, I read one word: "Congratulations". That's all I needed to see.

The sum of it all

If you pass, you will feel extremely proud. You will want to celebrate your achievement. At last, you will have the privilege of placing the *NBCT* modicum after your name. You will be a *National Board Certified Teacher!*

If you do not pass the first time, remember—your scores may be more a reflection of how you *wrote* than of how you *teach*. The assessors do not know you. The process does not measure the influence you have had on hundreds of young lives. There could be many reasons you did not reach the magical 275. Perhaps family situations kept you from giving your best effort. Maybe you did not give the certification process enough time. Perhaps you needed a mentor or support group more than you thought, or perhaps you had an off day at the Assessment Center.

As you analyze your scores, ask yourself what made your *highest* scoring area good, and what made your *lowest* scoring area not as good? When you've had time to get over the scoring, put everything away for several weeks. When (not if) you come back to it, decide which entries you will redo to help you certify next time. Remember—when you certify, it will make no difference whether it was on the first, second, or third try. All that will matter is that you made it!

About the Author

Jerry Parks earned B.S., M.A., & Ed.S degrees in education from Eastern Kentucky University, and completed additional graduate work at the University of Kentucky. He became a *National Board Certified Teacher* in 2002, and has received numerous "Teacher of the Year" honors at the local, state, and national level. He is a regular speaker at *National Middle School Association* conferences, and is currently department chairman and instructor of social studies at Georgetown Middle School in Georgetown, Kentucky. Feel free to contact Jerry with any questions, concerns, or comments about this book at: *kidztchr7@hotmail.com*, or *jparks@scott.k12.ky.us*.

Dr. Parks has also published two other books. His first, *With Joseph in the University of Adversity: The Mizraim Principles* is based on principles from the life of Joseph the Hebrew in the Old Testament. His second book, *Teacher Under Construction: Things I Wish I'd Known*, is a handbook to help new middle school teachers in their first year of teaching.

Jerry is currently Kentucky Regional Coordinator for the *National Board for Professional Teaching Standards*.

978-0-595-32728-7
0-595-32728-1

Printed in the United States
31999LVS00004B/487-492